PECOS BILL

ADAPTED BY
STEPHEN KRENSKY

ILLUSTRATIONS BY
PAUL TONG

M Millbrook Press/Minneapolis

Millbrook Press, Inc.
A division of Lerner Publishing Group
241 First Avenue North
Minneapolis, MN 55401

Website address: www.lernerbooks.com

Library of Congress Cataloging-in-Publication Data

Krensky, Stephen.
    Pecos Bill / by Stephen Krensky ; illustrations by Paul Tong. (Rev. ed.)
      p.   cm. — (On my own folklore)
    Summary: Relates some of the exploits of Pecos Bill, the extraordinary cowboy who was raised by coyotes, rode a mountain lion, and used a rattlesnake as a rope.
    ISBN-13: 978–1–57505–889–4 (lib. bdg. : alk. paper)
    ISBN-10: 1–57505–889–8 (lib. bdg. : alk. paper)
    1. Pecos Bill (Legendary character)—Legends. [1. Pecos Bill (Legendary character)—Legends. 2. Folklore—United States. 3. Tall tales.] I. Tong, Paul, ill. II. Title. III. Series: Krensky, Stephen. On my own folklore.
PZ8.1.K8663Pe 2007
398.2—dc22   2005033174

Manufactured in the United States of America
1 2 3 4 5 6 .– JR – 12 11 10 09 08 07

for my adventurous friend, Jim Storer
—S.K.

for Leigh and Donna,
my inspiration and support
—P.T.

Pecos Bill: A Folklore Hero

Maybe you have heard of Pecos Bill. Perhaps someone has mentioned his name, or you have heard a story. Pecos Bill is one of America's tall-tale heroes. Legend has it that Pecos Bill was the greatest cowboy who ever lived.

We call stories like Pecos Bill's tall tales because everything in them is extra big, extra fast, and extra wild. And the truth in these stories might be just a bit stretched. The heroes and heroines in tall tales are as tall as buildings, as strong as oxen, or as fast as lightning. They meet with wild adventures at every turn. But that's okay, because they can solve just about every problem that comes their way.

Tall tales may be funny and outsized. But they describe the life that many workers and pioneers shared. The people in these stories often have jobs that real people had. And the stories are always set in familiar places.

The first tellers of these tales may have known these people and places. Or they may have wished they could be just like the hero in the story. The stories were told again and again and passed from person to person. We call such spoken and shared stories folklore.

Folklore is the stories and customs of a place or a people. Folklore can be folktales like the tall tale. These stories are usually not written down until much later, after they have been told and retold for many years. Folklore can also be sayings, jokes, and songs.

Folklore can teach us something. A rhyme or a song may help us remember an event from long ago. Or it may just be for fun, such as a good ghost story or a jump-rope song. Folklore can also tell us about the people who share the stories.

Pecos Bill's story tells us about Texas and the Old Southwest. And it shows how cowboys and cowgirls captured our imagination. As the cowboy hero, Pecos Bill has the adventurous spirit of the West. Tales of his deeds quickly spread across the country. And we tell his story still.

Young Bill

Pecos Bill was born into a family
that liked wide open spaces.
He had lots of brothers and sisters—
sixteen or seventeen at least.

They all lived in East Texas.
The land there was so wide that
the sun spent the whole morning
crossing from one side to the other.

But then one day,
some new neighbors moved in.
They were 50 miles away,
but that was still too close.
"It's getting crowded
around here,"
said Bill's father.
"You're right," his mother said.
"Feels like people are looking
over your shoulder."
So they loaded up their wagon
and headed west.

It was a pretty bumpy ride.
Bill liked to sit way at the back,
bouncing up and down.
Sometimes the bumps came quicker
than snorts from a hungry hog.

One day, they crossed the Pecos River.
Bill was leaning out a bit too far,
and a bump knocked him
clear out of the wagon.
Bill so enjoyed taking such a tumble
that he forgot to cry out.
And no one else noticed
what had happened.

Except the coyotes.

They came sniffing around soon enough,

snapping and growling.

They expected Bill to be scared silly.

But Bill wasn't scared at all.

The biggest coyote snarled right at him,

showing two rows of sharp teeth.

Bill only laughed—

and snarled right back.

The coyotes were impressed,
so they adopted Bill into their pack.
They taught him their secrets,
like how to scratch behind his shoulder
and the best way to howl at the moon.

The coyotes always traveled together.

But every now and then,

Bill went out exploring by himself.

One day a cowboy came along.

Bill was wrestling

a couple of grizzly bears.

"Need any help?" the cowboy called out.

"Not really," said Bill,

"but I'm happy for the company."

He gave the bears
a particularly fierce look,
and they bounded away.

"I'll bet you've never seen a coyote
take on two bears before," said Bill.
"I still haven't," said the cowboy.
"What do you mean?" asked Bill.
"Well," said the cowboy,
"you're not a coyote.
You're a human being, same as me."

Bill shook his head.

"I've got fleas," he said,

"and I howl at the moon."

The cowboy shrugged.

"If that's all it takes to be a coyote,

then almost everyone I know

would be one too."

"Besides," the cowboy added,

"if you're a coyote, where's your tail?"

Now Bill had never looked for his tail.

He had just assumed it was there.

But now that he did look,

it was plain enough

that he didn't have one.

"What do you know?"

he said in surprise.

Maybe he was a human being after all.

Bill Finds Himself Some Company

Now that Bill knew he was human,
he set out to learn
all he could about people.
It wasn't long before he could outeat,
outdrink, outsleep, and outsnore
anyone for miles around.

20

But Bill wasn't satisfied yet.
He had spent enough time alone
already in his young life.
Now he wanted some company.
He had heard of a tough gang of riders
who were holed up in a canyon
a few days away.
So he set out to find them.

The first day out,
Bill's horse slipped and broke its leg.
Bill had to go on alone,
his saddle slung over his shoulder.
But he hadn't gone far
when a 10-foot rattlesnake
blocked his path, ready for a fight.

To be fair, Bill let the snake
have the first three bites.
Then he twisted the snake
this way and that
and tied it into a bow.
The rattler yelled for mercy.
Bill decided to let it go.
The rattler was so thankful
that he followed Bill from
then on.

Bill and the rattler made good progress

until a mountain lion

jumped off a cliff

and landed on Bill's neck.

This creature was bigger

than three steers put together.

But Bill didn't worry about such things.

In a minute, the fur was flying
on both sides.
The two kicked up so much dust,
it blotted out the sun.
But after Bill pinned the mountain lion
for the third time,
the lion gave up.

Bill saddled up the mountain lion
and coiled the rattlesnake like a rope.
The three of them went on from there,
sometimes leaping
100 feet at a time
just for fun.

The gang of riders
were just sitting down to breakfast
when Bill arrived.
He screeched and
whooped up a storm.
The mountain lion and the snake
hummed in the background.

The cowboys just sat there,

saying less than nothing.

So Bill helped himself

to beans and coffee.

Then he wiped his mouth

on a prickly pear cactus.

"Who's the boss around here?"

he asked.

A big fellow about eight feet tall

stood up.

His belt bristled

with pistols and knives.

He looked hard at the rattlesnake

and the mountain lion

and at old Bill himself.

"That was me, sir," he said.

"But you're the boss now."

The World's Greatest Cowboy

Now that Pecos Bill had a gang,
he needed a new horse to ride.
The gang had heard of one—
a wild stallion up in the mountains.
"Some call him Lightning," they said.
"He's the fastest, strongest
horse in the world."

Bill went off searching for Lightning.
And when he finally found him,
Lightning led Bill on a chase.
They went north to the Arctic Circle
and south to the bottom
of the Grand Canyon.
Lightning was boxed in at last,
and Bill jumped up on his back.

Lightning bucked Bill

across three states

but didn't throw him once.

Then Bill sang out a song

he had learned from the coyotes.

It praised Lightning's

strength and beauty.

By the time Bill was done singing,
Lightning had stopped bucking.
Bill offered to set the horse free,
but Lightning chose to stay.
He wasn't much tamer, though.
He liked dynamite mixed in with his hay,
and that gave him the kick of 10 mules.

Bill and Lightning led the gang
across Texas to round up steers.
But the men complained a lot.
Steers could be stubborn.
Collecting them was hard work.

Then Bill had an idea.

He snuck up on a longhorn and

let loose a rip-snorting coyote howl.

He scared it right out of its skin.

The embarrassed bull ran off

to grow a new coat.

And Bill cut its hide into thin strips,

which his men used as the first lassos.

After that, Bill and his cowboys

had an easier time moving their herds.

But it was still hard work

driving the cattle back and forth

between the summer and winter ranges.

So Bill did something about it.

He built the Perpetual Motion Ranch

on Pinnacle Peak.

The ranch tilted back and forth.

One side stayed far to the north.

The other reached deep to the south.

Once the place was fenced off,

the cattle could wander back and forth

on their own.

The only problem was how steep

the tilt got at times.

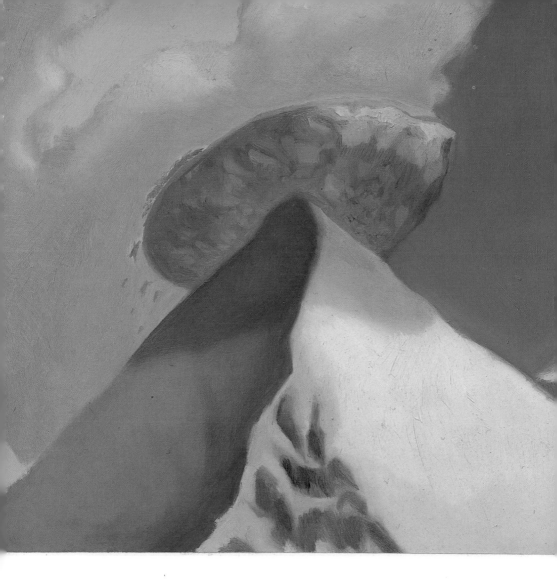

When the cattle bunched at one end,

they often fell off

trying to head back the other way.

Bill solved this problem by raising steers
with short legs on one side of their bodies.
Even a strong wind couldn't move them
when their short legs were standing uphill.
Now the men had more time to catch strays.
And when that was done,
they caught up on their sleep.

Settling Down

As exciting as Bill's life was,
he was getting a little bored
until the day he rode
the Oklahoma cyclone.
It came roaring down from Kansas,
and Bill jumped aboard just for fun.
Well, that cyclone went ripping
and roaring along.
It knocked down mountains
and shredded trees like matchsticks.
When it saw it couldn't throw Bill,
it just rained out from under him.
Bill fell down fast,
landing with a splash
in a fast-moving river.

He shook the water out of his eyes,

And what did he see?

A girl was riding by, standing on a catfish.

Sluefoot Sue was her name.

Bill was quite impressed

with what she was doing

because he hadn't thought of it first.

Now Bill was never at a loss for words
until he met Sluefoot Sue.
He was so tongue-tied at first,
it took him most of a day
just to get the knot out.
Sue felt the same way right back at him.
It wasn't long
before they decided to get hitched.

Sue had two requests for her wedding.
Her wedding dress should have
a fashionable steel-spring bustle.
And she wanted to ride Lightning to the ceremony.
On their wedding day, Bill helped Sue up
onto Lightning's saddle.

Now Lightning liked Sue,

but he didn't take to the bustle.

He bucked once and blasted Sue up into space.

She fell back to earth landing right on her bustle.

Then she bounced right up into space again.

Over and over,

Bill tried to catch Sue on the bounce.

And over and over, he missed.

He finally lassoed a tornado

to help him catch up with her.

They sailed through the storm
until it ran out of steam in California.
Much to Bill's surprise,
they landed on top of his parents' wagon.
Bill could hardly believe it.
His ma and pa still hadn't found
a place to settle down.
"Come back to Texas," he told them.
"There ain't a prettier place
between here and the moon."

So everyone returned to Bill's ranch.
They put down roots so deep
that some of them
popped out as trees in China.
And his family lives in Texas still,
herding cattle and telling tales
of days gone by.

Further Reading and Websites

American Folklore
> http://www.americanfolklore.net
> This folklore website features tall tales, ghost stories, regional legends, and famous characters.

Gibbons, Gail. *Cowboys and Cowgirls.* New York: Little, Brown and Company, 2003. Illustrated with original watercolors, this book provides a historical introduction to life on the range.

Markel, Rita. *Your Travel Guide to America's Old West.* Minneapolis: Lerner Publications Company, 2002. Markel prepares readers for a trip back in time to the Old West, with recommendations on what to wear, how to get around, local customs and manners, and other tips.

Morley, Jacqueline. *How Would You Survive in the American West?* New York: Franklin Watts, 1997. Morley explores all the hazards, hard work, and excitement involved in trekking west in a wagon.

Pelta, Kathy. *Texas.* Minneapolis: Lerner Publications Company, 2002. This book covers the region's Native American culture, the settlement of the wild frontier, and the growth of the state.